# First Edition

## Genuine Autographed Collectible

---

Do you want me to sign it in ink or in lipstick?

Gift Card

**D**ate:

**T**o:

**F**rom:

**M**essage:

**What Do Books Do?**

## BOOKS ARE POWERFUL!

**Books Educate!**
**Books Enlighten!**
**Books Empower!**
**Books Emancipate!**
**Books Entertain!**
**Books Spring Eternal!**
**Books Drive Exploration!**
**Books Spark Evolution!**
**Books Ignite Revolution!**

Sharon Esther Lampert

**Most Frequently Asked Sexiest Question** (microaggression)

Ardent male fan: "Great poem! Did you write that poem all by yourself?"

My response: "I stole all the words from the dictionary!"

# I
# Stole
# All
# The
# Words
# From
# The
# Dictionary

**KADIMAH PRESS**
*Gifts of Genius*

Literature, Poetry, Education, Creativity, Art, Genius, Sharon Esther Lampert

## I STOLE ALL THE WORDS FROM THE DICTIONARY
Sharon Esther Lampert is One of the World's Greatest Poets

©2024 ©2022 by Sharon Esther Lampert. All Rights Reserved.
No part of this book may be used or reproduced in any manner whatsoever without written permission except in the case of brief quotations embodied in critical articles and reviews.

## KADIMAH PRESS: GIFTS OF GENIUS
Books may be purchased for education, business, or sales promotional use.

ISBN Hardcover: 978-1-885872-06-7
ISBN Paperback: 978-1-885872-07-4
ISBN E-Book: 978-1-885872-08-1
Library of Congress Catalog Card Number: 2022911276

Fan Mail:
Website: www.SharonEstherLampert.com
Email: FANS@SharonEstherLampert.com

For Global Online Orders and Distribution:
INGRAM 1 Ingram Blvd. La Vergne, TN 37086-3629
Phone: 615-793-5000, Fax orders: 615-287-6990

Age 9
**THE QUEEN HAS ARRIVED!**
"My daughter is a poet, philosopher, and teacher. She is the Princess & the Pea!
**BEAUTY & BRAINS!"**
**MOMMY**
**XOXO**

## LOVE OF MY LIFETIME: MOMMY EVE PAIKOFF LAMPERT

Book Design and Interior: Prodigy Sharon Esther Lampert

Editor: Dave Segal

## First Edition

Manufactured in the United States of America

## Dedication
## Philip Winters
Every typo is your fault — not mine!

"**One great poem** is lucky.
**Two great poems** mean I have something,
but I don't know what it is.
**Three great poems** mean I have something,
and I have to learn to work it — but there is
no instruction manual.
**Forty great poems** mean I have a gift,
and the gift is a mystery."
—**Sharon Esther Lampert**

# LITERATURE IS POWERFUL BEYOND WORDS FOR IT CREATES WORLDS

**Sharon Esther Lampert**
**P**oet, **P**rophet, **P**hilosopher, **P**eacemaker, **P**aladin of Education, **P**rodigy

# FAN MAIL
## FANS@SharonEstherLampert.com

# A PHENOMENON...
## SHARON ESTHER LAMPERT

Lithe and lovely ... like a fawn.
This lady fascinates me ... from dusk till dawn.
Feminine and comely ... she's beyond belief
A blue-beam from her eyes ... is my soothing relief.

Girlish in her braces ... maidenly in her style
I yearn for her embraces ... and adore her friendly smile.
As tasteful as any artist ... you'll ever see
She's a compendium of class ... from A to Z.

If you'd like to see a figure, that puts Venus to shame
Behold her in a swimsuit, and your passions will aflame.
Ever exuding goodness . . . guided from above
Miss Sharon is the essence, and epitome of Love.

She's the inspiration of sages, and also fools like me
And the most magnificent female, I'm sure I'll ever see.
The nights are now endearing, & never filled with doubt
I sometimes wake up singing, cause it's Sharon . . .
I dream about.

Affectionately, . .
A devoted fan,
—Harry McVeety

## SEE THE WORLD THROUGH THE EYES OF A CREATIVE GENIUS

### EIGHTEEN POETRY BOOKS
3 Editions: Hardcover, Paperback, and E-Book

#### The Greatest Poems Ever Written on Extraordinary World Events

1. I Stole All the Words From The Dictionary
2. **IMMORTALITY IS MINE**: Greatest Poems Ever Written on Extraordinary World Events
3. **POETRY JEWELS:** **D**iamonds, **E**meralds, **S**apphires, **R**ubies, and **P**earls
4. **V.E.S.S.E.L.** **V**ery. **E**xtra. **S**pecial. **S**haron. **E**sther. **L**ampert.
5. Does Your Kid Read Sharon Esther Lampert?
6. Does Your Professor Teach Reason-N-Rhyme?
7. What Happens When You Dress Up Albert Einstein as Marilyn Monroe?
8. Sharon Esther Lampert: The Sexiest Creative Genius in Human History
9. **SEA IN, SEE OUT:** - Childhood Poem
10. **CUPID:** Language of Love — Written in Letter **C**
11. Spiraling Downward, Upward We Stand United: 911 World Trade Center Tragedy
12. In 5 Minutes, Learn 5000 Years of Jewish History
13. Love Ever Reborn Is Love Ever Newborn
14. It's Not Easy Being a **JEWISH SEX SYMBOL** But Someone Has to Do It!
    Poems Written About Sharon Esther Lampert by Her Ardent Fans
15. **SWEET NOTHINGS:** Love Portraits in Poetry
16. Witches, Whores, Wives, and Writers
17. No **F**akes! No **F**lops! No **F**illers! No **F**at! No **F**-Bomb!
18. 7 Practice Husbands

• Buy Autographed Books Online

• All Global Bookstores: USA, CAN, UK, AUS, ASIA, AFRICA, INDIA, and MIDDLE EAST

# Table of Contents

### POPULAR POEMS
- POETREE ... p. 1
- RESTLESS SUNRISE ... p. 2
- BE BORN ... p. 3
- WORLD PEACE EQUATION ... p. 4
- TRUE LOVE ... p. 5
- BE ART ... p. 5
- THE 22 COMMANDMENTS ... p. 7
- How to Read a Poem by Sharon Esther Lampert ... p. 9
- 10 Poetry Reading Tips ... p. 13

### THE GREATEST POEMS EVER WRITTEN ON EXTRAORDINARY WORLD EVENTS

### PORTRAITS IN POETRY
- THE DELIVERER: Nelson Mandela ... p. 8
- A SURVIVOR'S BURDEN: Nazi Hunter Simon Wiesenthal ... p. 21

### JEWISH HOLOCAUST POEM for Mandatory Holocaust Education
- A SURVIVOR'S BURDEN Nazi Hunter Simon Wiesenthal and FAN MAIL ... p. 21

### EXTRAORDINARY WORLD EVENTS
- EDUCATE NOT ... p. 11
- The Militant Palestinian Toddler Terrorist ... p. 12
- TSUNAMI ... p. 13
- ARAB SPRING: Tahrir Square Insanity ... p.14
- HAITI: Crimes of Insanity Against Humanity ... p. 15
- STOP CAMPUS RAPE ... p. 17
- Central Park, Water Fight, Flight & Tears and FAN MAIL ... p. 19
- RUN SAID RABBI ... p. 47

### FEMINIST POEMS
- BE HARD, FASTER, and MINUS ZERO WOMAN ... p. 16
- STOP CAMPUS RAPE ... p. 17
- Central Park, Water Fight, Flight & Tears and FAN MAIL ... p. 19

### LOVE POEMS
- FIRST LOVE ... p. 4
- RABBI ARI ... p. 22 (rhyme)
- FIRST LOVE ... p. 23
- THAT KISS ... p. 24 (rhyme)
- MY MAN ... p. 25

### 2024 ADDITIONS:
FAN MAIL ... p. 48
DEADICATION ... p. 49
DUMB DEE DEE DUMB DUMB ... p. 51

### SEE THE WORLD THOUGH THE EYES OF A CREATIVE GENIUS
- About Prodigy Sharon Esther Lampert ... pp. 26-28
- One of the World's Greatest Poets ... p. 29
- The Sexiest Creative Genius in Human History ... p. 37
- FAN MAIL ... pp. 31-37
- Gazillions of National and International Poetry Publications ... pp. 38-39
- World Famous Quotes ... pp. 40-41
- KADIMAH PRESS: Gifts of Genius ... pp. 42-43
- Count Your Blessings. Practice Gratitude ... p. 44

# SEE THE WORLD THROUGH THE

## SHARON ESTHER LAMPERT

The Greatest Poems Ever Written on Extraordinary World Events

# EYES OF A CREATIVE GENIUS

## WARNING

**KEEP A SAFE DISTANCE OF 6 FEET**
**HIGH LEVELS OF INTENSITY**
**INTELLECTUAL COMBUSTION**

### SHARON ESTHER LAMPERT

## PRODIGY

POET, PHILOSOPHER, PROPHET, PEACEMAKER,
PALADIN OF EDUCATION, PHOTON SUPERHERO
PIONEER, PERFORMER, PUBLISHER, PLAYER
PRESIDENT, PHOENIX, PRINCESS of ISRAEL

# Unleash The Creator The God Within

I was born gifted. It is a gift that keeps giving!
I refer to my extra-body part as my "**C**reative **A**pparatus."

My gift is my most important relationship, my most rewarding relationship,
and paradoxically, my most difficult relationship:

**EXCITING! EXHILERATING! ELECTRIFYING! EXHAUSTING!**

I awake in the middle of a sleepless night and
write the whole book! — There are no rough drafts!

I am not an I — I am a WE — and a They!

My gift did not come with an instruction manual.

There were no teachers to guide me, and no classes
to teach how to maximize my creative potential.

Intuitive gifts of insight, imagination, and vision cannot be taught in school.

I am its servant and messenger, and the instrument of its desires and destiny!

## Sharon Esther Lampert

**SEE THE WORLD THROUGH THE EYES OF A CREATIVE GENIUS**

**P**oet, **P**hilosopher, **P**rophet, **P**eacemaker, **P**rincess & **P**ea, **P**aladin of Education, and **P**rodigy

# 10 Poetry Reading Tips

1. Begin reading the poem to yourself silently.

2. Become familiar with the poem.

3. Read the poem by feeling and following the rhythm.

4. Take note of words needing emphasis.

5. Take note of places to pause.

6. Get to know the poem well.

7. Read the poem aloud in a natural voice.

8. Read the poem for surface meaning.

9. Reread the poem for the larger meaning of underlying ideas and depths of emotional power.

10. After reading the poem, reflect silently.

"The Sole Intention of My Poetry is to Add LIGHT to Your Soul"

"Food is for the Body
Education is for the Mind
Poetry is for the Soul"

"I AM an OPEN Book, to KNOW ME is to READ ME"

"Every Thought in Your Head Was Put There by a Writer"

"When I'm not Writing I'm Reading. When I'm not Writing or Reading, I'm Singing."

"Please Don't Let Me Die with a Typo!"

# POE**T**REE

Ink needs a Pen
Pen needs Paper
Paper needs a Poem
Poem needs a Poet
Poet needs a Muse
Muse needs a Poet
Poet needs Divine Inspiration
Divine Inspiration needs Divine Intervention
Divine Intervention needs Divine Grace
Divine Grace needs Immortality
Immortality needs Eternity
Eternity needs Readers of Poetry

—Sharon Esther Lampert

@All Rights Reserved. Sharon Esther Lampert.

# The Restless Sunrise

**A Streaming Golden Light
Enters In and Under the Windowsill**

**A Restless Sleeper
Is Awakened to New Beginnings**

**To Catch a Sunrise
The Dreamer Arises as the Light Bursts Forth**

**The Sunrise Lights Up the Sky
In Anticipation of a World**

**That Has Yet To Be Created.**

—Sharon Esther Lampert

@All Rights Reserved. Sharon Esther Lampert.

# BE BORN

Be Born.
Become Educated.
Love Your Work.
Make a Meaningful Contribution—
to Yourself, Your Family, and Humanity.
Be a True Friend to Yourself First.
Have Sex with Someone You Love.
Make Love with Complete Abandon.
Enjoy Unconditional Love from Your Devoted Pet.
Make Time to Read the Funnies and Laugh.
Save Enough Money to Visit the Popular,
Pretty, and Peaceful Places of the World.
Read Great Literature, Listen to Great Music,
See Great Art, Watch the Great Movies,
Play the Fun Sports, and Dance till Dawn.
Taste the Great Culinary Delights of the World—
Eat Slowly, Enjoy Every Bite, and Stay in Shape.
Plan One Great Adventure and Stick to the Plan.
Grow Old and Wise.
Leave Your Money to Someone
You Love—Who Loves You Back.
Die in Your Sleep.

—Sharon Esther Lampert

Find the Light and Live in the Light

@All Rights Reserved. Sharon Esther Lampert.

**#1 Poetry Website for Student Projects**

# WORLD PEACE EQUATION
## VG+VL=VP

Virtue of the Good + Value of Life = Vision of Peace

### The Mathematical and Philosophical Proof for World Peace

$$VG + VL = VP$$
$$VP = VG + VL$$
$$VP = V(G+L)$$
$$P = (G+L)$$

Peace = Good + Life

Peace = Good Life

Gift Shop: WorldPeaceEquation.com

@All Rights Reserved. Peacemaker Sharon Esther Lampert.com

# True Love

True Love is Unconditional.
True Love is Found in the Deed.
True Love is Found in the We.
True Love Joins the Heart,
Mind, and Body as One.

By Sharon Esther Lampert

# BE ART

ART IS SMART
ART IS OF THE HEART
MAKE ART NOT WAR
YOU ARE BORN FOR GREATNESS
YOR ARE A MASTERPIECE

SHARON ESTHER LAMPERT
www.sharonestherlampert.com

@All Rights Reserved. Sharon Esther Lampert.

# YOU HAD TO OUTDO MOSES!

## Moses Has 10 Commandments. You Have 22 Commandments!

—Joel Rapplefeld

# SHARON ESTHER LAMPERT
# 8TH PROPHETESS OF ISRAEL

## The 8 Prophetesses of Israel

**Sarah**
Ageless Beauty, Seer, Holy Spirit
- Genesis 17:15-17:27
- Genesis 18:1-18:15
- Genesis 21:1-21:22
- Genesis 23:1-23:20

**Miriam**
Saved the life of Moses
- Exodus 2:1-2:10
- Exodus 15:20-15:27
- Numbers 12:1-12:16
- Numbers 20:1-20:6

**Deborah**
Warrior and 4th Judge
- Judges 4:4-4:14
- Judges 5:1-5:31

**Hannah**
Personal Prayer
- 1 Samuel 1:1-1:28

**Abigail**
Prophecy of King David
- 1 Samuel 25:2-25:44
- 1 Samuel 27:1-27:3
- 1 Samuel 30:4
- 2 Samuel 2:2
- 2 Samuel 3:2

**Huldah**
Learning, Enlightenment, and Peace
- 2 Kings 22:1-20

**Esther**
Rescued Jews from Genocide
- Esther 2:7-2:23
- Esther 4:1-4:16
- Esther 5:1-5:8
- Esther 7:1-7:10
- Esther 8:3-8:8
- Esther 9:12-9:14
- Esther 9:26-9:32

**Sharon Esther Lampert**
- 22 Commandments
- World Peace Equation
- 40 Absolute Truths
- World Poetry Record
- 40 Universal Gold Standards of Education
- 22 Steps to Find a Soulmate
- 10 Thinking Tools of Creative Genius

# All You Will Ever Need to Know About God
# The 22 Commandments
A Universal Moral Compass For All People, For All Religions, and For All Time

1. **LIFE**
Over Death

2. **STRENGTH**
Over Weakness

3. **DEED**
Over Sin

4. **LOVE**
Over Hatred

5. **TRUTH**
Over Lie

6. **WISDOM**
Over Stupidity

7. **OPTIMISM**
Over Pessimism

8. **SHARING**
Over Selfishness

9. **PRAISE**
Over Criticism

10. **LOYALTY**
Over Abandonment

11. **RESPONSIBILITY**
Over Blame

12. **GRATITUDE**
Over Envy

13. **REWARD**
Over Punishment

14. **DEMOCRACY**
Over Domination

15. **CREATION**
Over Destruction

16. **EDUCATION**
Over Ignorance

17. **COOPERATION**
Over Competition

18. **FREEDOM**
Over Oppression

19. **COMPASSION**
Over Indifference

20. **FORGIVENESS**
Over Revenge

21. **PEACE**
Over War

22. **JOY**
Over Suffering

"Moses had 10 commandments. You have 22 commandments. You had to out do Moses."
Joel Rapplefeld

"Inside Every Jewish Person Is a Little Moses Tying to Get Out."
Chabad Rabbi Ben Tzion Krasnianski

Sharon Esther Lampert
# KADIMAH
8TH Prophetess of Israel

Learn It. Live It. Share It.

---

1. Sarah: (Genesis 21:12)
Ageless Beauty, Seer, Holy Spirit

2. Miriam: Exodus 15:21
Saved the life of Moses

3. Devorah: Judges 4:4
Warrior and 4th Judge

4. Chanah: I Samuel 2:1-10
Personal Prayer

5. Abigail: I Samuel (25:2-44)
Prophecy of King David

6. Huldah: Kings 22:14
Learning, Enlightenment, and Peace

7. Esther: The Book of Esther
Saved the Jews from Genocide

8. Kadimah: 22 Commandments
Beauty, Seer, Holy Spirit, Learning, Englightenment and World Peace

@All Rights Reserved. Sharon Esther Lampert.

My gifts did not come with an instruction manual. There were no teachers to guide me, and no classes to teach how to maximize my creative potential. I am its servant and messenger, and the instrument of its desires and destiny!

## Sharon Esther Lampert

**P**oet
**P**rophet
**P**hilosopher
**P**aladin of Education
**P**eacemaker
**P**rincess Kadimah
**P**rodigy

# How to Read a Poem by Sharon Esther Lampert

### 1. Sharon's Poetry Paintings
Similar to the poet William Blake, her poems are accompanied by elaborate visual graphics that enrich and compliment the text. The poems are wall hangings, and her poems are framed by ardent fans and hang in their living spaces, like paintings. Students, the world over, read her poems in their classrooms, and use her poetry for their school assignments.

### 2. Sharon is a Master of Condensation
Sharon is a master of the art of condensation. She is able to condense a major world event in world history into a one-page poem. Her immortal literary gems come in a variety of lengths: A single sentence, a single page, and grand sweeping epics.

### 3. Sharon Is a Literary Photographer
Her poems are telescopic of the main event and microscopic of the infinite details.

### 4. Sharon Can Pack a Single Verse
Sharon's poems are known for her ability to weave poetry, philosophy, and comedy into a single verse.

### 5. Documentary Poet: Poems are Cinematic Journey's Through History
Sharon's poems take you on a cinematic journey, and make you feel as if you are reliving the event, as if it happened today.

### 6. Sharon's Poems Are Completed Literary Works
Many poets leave abandoned poems that went unfinished. Sharon's poems are completed works of art. Every word is essential to the poem. You cannot remove or replace a word. There are no extra words. Every word has its rightful place and fits to perfection.

### 7. Sharon's Poems Are All Inspired Works of Art
All of her poems are inspired. There are no rough drafts. Like giving birth to a baby, the poem incubates in her extra-body part a "Creative Apparatus" and is birthed in minutes. Like a baby, the poems are delivered whole and complete.

### 8. Sharon's Signature Endings: The Epiphany (Spiritual Illumination)
Quote: "The Sole Intention of My Poetry Is to Add LIGHT to Your Soul"
The last verse of every poem delivers a message that educates, enlightens, and empowers. Her searing signature endings find their way into your heart, open your mind to a deeper understanding, and stay with you forever.

©2000. All Rights Reserved. Sharon Esther Lampert.
FAN MAIL: FANS@SharonEstherLampert.com

#1 Poetry Website for Student Projects    BLACK LIVES MATTER

# www.WorldFamousPoems.com
## The Greatest Poems Ever Written on Extraordinary World Events

Sharon Esther Lampert
8TH Prophetess of Israel
Enlightenment: 24 Commandments
**THE DELIVERER**

First Responder Poet
December 10 2013

"Food Is for the Body,
Education Is for the Mind,
And Poetry Is for the Soul."
Sharon Esther Lampert

## A Tribute to Nelson Mandela
## THE DELIVERER
### An Enemy and Head of State

By Sharon Esther Lampert

A difference, can one life make.
A PhD. in Freedom Fighter.

A delicate balance, a work in progress.
A coexistence, a sharing of resources.

Might does not make right.
White skin is not a privilege.

Damned if you do, damned if you don't:
Violent coup or peaceful non-cooperation?

Deliver yourself from ignorance.
Enlightenment is a long walk to freedom.

Don't die in vain, learn from your mistakes.
The **BLAME GAME** is not a solution to a problem.

Tit for Tat: All Evil Is Justified.
Two wrongs don't make a right.

Choose democracy over fascism.
Choose integration over segregation.

Choose shareholders over domination.
Choose forgiveness over revenge.

**CAST YOUR VOTE 4 HOPE
EDUCATE: MIND, BODY, AND SPIRIT**

MANDIBA
Rolihlahla
Dalibhunga
Mandela
46664

MOSES
Walk to Freedom: 40 Years
Enlightenment: Ten Commandments
**THE DELIVERER**

Martin Luther King
Enlightenment: I Have a Dream
**THE DELIVERER**

Choose nurture over nature: **LOVE, PEACE,** and **UNDERSTANDING.**
Choose the future over the past. **BE PRESENT.**

Be born in apartheid (1948-1994) and fight for **EQUALITY.**
**EMANCIPATION:** Be told you're a nobody and die a somebody special.

There are good people and there are bad people, and
**THERE IS NO OTHER DIFFERENCE.**
Good People: Nothing Is a Problem ... Bad People: Everything Is a Problem

Be guided by your hopes, not your fears.
See future generations: **"THE BORN FREES."**

The Sole Intention of My Poetry Is to Add **LIGHT** to Your Soul

"For to be free is not merely to cast off one's chains, but to live in a way that respects and enhances the freedom of others." N. Mandela

# EDUCATE NOT

**No Time to Teach:**
In Class, They Give a General Overview.
On Tests, They Want Particular Details.

**No Time to Learn:**
All By Myself, I Got to Teach Myself a Zillion Facts:
I Got No Study Skills, I Got No Tutor,
The First Day of School, I Gotta Be Behind.

**Students Got a Cheat-Sheet:**
I Use Citations From Books
I Got No Time to Read.

**Teachers Got a Cheat Sheet:**
They Got No Time to Read IT.
They Weigh IT:
Looks Beautiful
They Grade IT A.
Looks Pretty
They Grade IT B.
Looks OK
They Grade IT C.
Looks Ugly
They Grade IT D.
Looks Can Kill
They Grade IT F.

**Quantity Over Quality:**
Education System is Dumb
And is Gonna Get Dumber,
Wastes My Good Dime,
My Good Mind,
And My Good Time.
I Survive, I Don't Thrive.

Facts Move From Textbook
To Blackboard to Notebook.
Gotta Get the Facts **INSIDE OF ME:**
No Time to Think,
No Time to Write an Outline,
No Time for Research,
No Time to Write a Rough Draft,
No Time to Reread, Revise, and Rewrite,
No Time to Write a Final Draft,
No TIme to Write My Masterpiece.
When I Get IT Back, My Work-In-Progress,
I Trash IT. I Got No Time for Junk.

Teachers Got No Time to Teach.
I Got No Time to Learn.
No Time to Educate.
**EDUCATE NOT.**

By Sharon Esther Lampert
**Creative Genius**
www.WorldFamousPoems.com

@All Rights Reserved. Sharon Esther Lampert.

# WORLD FAMOUS POEMS
## The Greatest Poems Ever Written on Extraordinary World Events

2009: Wrote Poem
2016: SON OF HAMAS autographed poem
2023: SON OF HAMAS sent poem to network

www.WorldFamousPoems.com

On March 31, 2016 I had the honor of meeting Mr. Yousef SON OF HAMAS SPY FOR ISRAEL in Boca Raton, Florida at Temple Beth-El and he autographed my poem — and I autographed his copy of my poem.

**Militant Palestinian Toddler Terrorist**
By Sharon Esther Lampert, 2009

At My Mother's Breast...
I learned how to thirst for the blood of Jews

Other toddlers learn how to live and love
I will learn how to hate Jews and die as a martyr

Other toddlers have parents that love them
My parents love to hate Jews

Other toddlers wear blue and pink
I wear a belt packed with explosives to kill Jews

Other toddlers love to cuddle adorable stuffed animals
I love to clench rocks to throw at Israeli soldiers

Other toddlers have a favorite blanket
I love to stomp on and burn American and Israeli flags

Other toddlers chant "Baby Einstein" nursery rhymes
I chant political slogans, "Destroy Israel, Free Palestine!"

Other toddlers love to play funny games
I have a toy chest filled with katyusha rockets that make Jews cry

Today I plan to kill Jewish mothers and fathers, and tonight
WE WILL ALL BE TOGETHER IN HEAVEN

IN HEAVEN,
I will know the love of a Jewish mother and father
AND I WILL REST IN PEACE

The Sole Intention of My Poetry Is to Add LIGHT to Your Soul
Sharon Esther Lampert    FANS@SharonEstherLampert.com

SEE THE WORLD THROUGH THE EYES OF A CREATIVE GENIUS

- Prodigy
- Prophet
- Philosopher
- Poet
- Paladin of Education
- Peacemaker
- Princess Kadimah
- PHOTON SUPERHERO
- PINUP
- Princess & Pea
- Phoenix

SHARON ESTHER LAMPERT
**PRINCESS KADIMAH**
8TH PROPHETESS OF ISRAEL
**GOD IS GO! DO!**
THE 22 COMMANDMENTS

Like MOSES, MOSAB Wants to Deliver the Palestinians from Ideological Bondage

World Famous Poet Sharon Esther Lampert and SON OF HAMAS Mosab Hassan Yousef
THE GREEN PRINCE
March 31, 2016
Temple Beth-El
Boca Raton, Florida

## WORLD FAMOUS POEM
## TSUNAMI

How many tears can the ocean hold?
What the history books don't tell you
Is that the Indian Ocean was formed
By thousands of years of tears
That flowed from the fishermen of Sumatra.
Their pain was unbearable.
Their poverty was immeasurable.
Little to eat, little to wear,
Little to learn, too little work.
They were abandoned and forsaken.
Deep within their broken silent hearts,
An echo was heard.
The little earth quaked –
As it could no longer hold their tears.

Tens of thousands of tears overflowed
Deadly waves, crashing ashore
Sweeping their pain out from under
Their tattered rugs of impoverishment –
Out onto the front pages of newspapers worldwide.
Finally, the world took notice of their tears:
They sent care packages of food, clothing, shelter, schools, and cash.
They sent care packages of compassion, mercy, tolerance, and love.
The tears of the fisherman brought new life to tens of thousands in pain.
Salty, salty, sea water, tears of the fallen.
Salty, salty, sea water, heals the wounds of grief.
What the history books don't tell you is
How many tears can a human heart hold
Before it cracks beneath the surface
From the strain and pain and swells open
And learns how to love.

Sharon Esther Lampert
Sexiest Creative Genius in Human History
© All Rights Reserved. January 29th, 2005
Todah Rabah to Karl, My Darling Muse

In memory of the victims in Indonesia, India, Sri Lanka, Thailand, Maldives, Somalia, and Myanmar. 200,000 people died.

#1 Poetry Website for Student Projects

# www.WorldFamousPoems.com

The Greatest Poems Ever Written on Extraordinary World Events

## Tahrir Square Insanity

Cairo, Egypt, February 1, 2011

"Innaharda, ehna kullina Misryeen!"

"Innaharda, ehna kullina Misryeen!"

Throw Rocks
Chant Slogans
Bow in Prayer

Bow in Prayer
Chant Slogans
Throw Rocks

"Innaharda, ehna kullina Misryeen!"

Chant Slogans
Throw Rocks
Bow in Prayer

Throw Rocks
Bow in Prayer
Chant Slogans

"Innaharda, ehna kullina Misryeen!"

"Innaharda, ehna kullina Misryeen!"

Chant Slogans
Bow in Prayer
Throw Rocks

Bow in Prayer
Throw Rocks
Chant Slogans

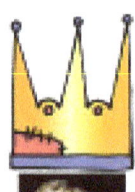

Sharon Esther Lampert
Poet
Philosopher
Paladin of Education
Peacemaker
Pioneer
PIN-UP and Prophet
Sexiest Creative Genius
in Human History
Princess Kadimah
The 8TH Prophetess of Israel
Books
Immortality is Mine
Poetry Jewels
Sweet Nothings
VESSEL

Political Injustice
Religious Intolerance
Sexual Discrimination

Democratic Reforms:
Free Speech
Civil Rights
Personal Liberty

"Today, We Are All Egyptians"

"Food Is for the Body,
Education Is for the Mind,
and Poetry Is for the Soul"
Sharon Esther Lampert

"The Sole Intention of My Poetry is to Add LIGHT to Your Soul"

@All Rights Reserved. Sharon Esther Lampert.

Haitian Earthquake, Port-Au-Prince, January 13, 2010

# Crimes of Insanity Against Humanity

An abandoned Haitian child wanders the streets alone.
His home is an archeological ruin of collectible fragments.
His family is buried alive, entrapped and entombed in rubble.
His ancestors are unearthed and cannot rest in peace.
His dog collects and chews on the bones.
His school is decimated and classmates are presumed dead.
His church cathedral is cracked, crushed, and crumbles.
His government palace is shattered, smashed, and splinters.
His hospital is defaced, disfigured, and devastated.
His prisoners are left unscathed, and are set free to use and abuse.
His God has forsaken them, cursed them, and destroyed them.
He is immeasurably heartbroken, humiliated, and hungry.
The earth continues to shake, rattle, and roll underneath his calloused feet.

Text ten dollars to the Red Cross.
Save one body from the rubble.
Save one leg from amputation.
Save one belly from hunger.
Save one heart from pain and suffering.
Save one voice to pray for forgiveness to the devil who is in the details.
Two wrongs don't make a right: Punish the sin, not the sinner.
God should be put on trial for crimes of insanity against humanity.
The earth continues to shake, rattle, and roll underneath their calloused feet.

We are all the living dead, awaiting our demise, our final destiny.
Pyrrhic victories. Time cannot heal us. Time hurts us. Time crushes us.
There is hell on earth and hell below the earth: We will never rest in peace.
Soon the rainy season will soak their tents, and soon after the hurricane season will level them.
Justice: God is put on trial, found guilty of all crimes against humanity, and declared insane.
Until then, the earth continues to shake, rattle, and roll underneath our calloused feet.

By Sharon Esther Lampert

@All Rights Reserved. Sharon Esther Lampert.

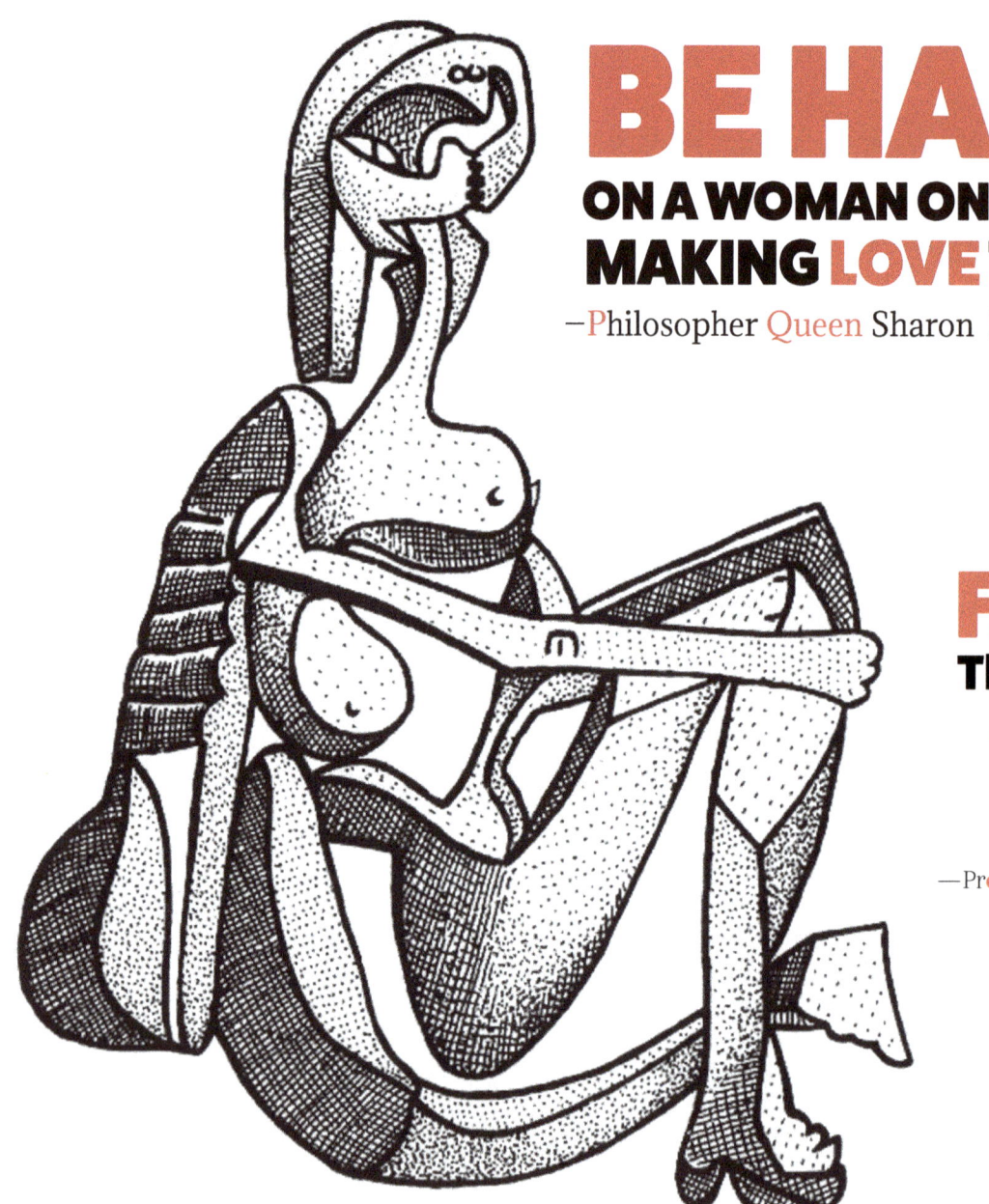

# BE HARD
## ON A WOMAN ONLY WHEN MAKING LOVE TO HER
—Philosopher Queen Sharon Esther Lampert

# FASTER
## Than Any Boy Anywhere Anytime Any Age
—Prodigy Sharon Esther Lampert

# MINUS ZERO WOMAN
## A WOMAN IS RAISED TO BELIEVE THAT WITHOUT A MAN SHE IS NOTHING ONLY TO FIND OUT THAT WITH A MAN SHE BECOMES LESS THAN NOTHING.

—Poet Sharon Esther Lampert

@All Rights Reserved. Sharon Esther Lampert.

# #1 Poetry Website for Student Projects

## SEE THE WORLD THROUGH THE EYES OF A CREATIVE GENIUS
## STOP CAMPUS RAPE

**S**tuds, **S**luts, **S**aints, **S**acrificial Lambs, **S**urvivors, **S**uicide, **S**emen, **S**candal, and **S**tigmata

By Prodigy Sharon Esther Lampert, October 29, 2015 (Final: Oct 24, 2016)

It is the first week of school
The class president invites her to a party

He plys me with alcohol (and drug**zzzzz**)
I don't even know his last name

He walks me home
I don't even remember his first name

I fall asleep in my bed
He **R**apes me

I wake up with him on top of me:
**Flight, fight or freeze?**
I hope he is wearing a condom?
I hope I'm not pregnant?
I hope I don't have a sexually transmitted
disease? I hope I'm not labeled, "**SLUT**"?

**STIGMATA:** I cry **R**APE kit
He cries foul: consensual sex

I scored a knockout punch
He scored a touch down

**STUD:** He brags to buddies of sexual conquest
I bawl to outraged parents who file a lawsuit

Boys post list of sexual conquests on wall: "**SLUTS**"
Girls carry **R**ape mattresses across campus (IVY: CU)

DNA speaks truth to power, **BUT** not in my case
Police don't prosecute **HE SAID, SHE SAID**

He won a Heisman Trophy; "**CAN DO NO WRONG**"
She's a **LIAR**: She wants a boyfriend not a booty call

**Obama's Administration Cri De Coeur: 1 Is 2 Many**
**SACRIFICIAL LAMB:** "Melia Obama Beer-Pong Incident"
**R** USA Secret Service fast asleep? (IVY: Brown U, 2015)

Lady Gaga belts out, "**Til It Happens to U**" (**R**aped at 19)
Oscar nominated co-writer Diane Warren **m**olested at 12

**RAPE:** Usually someone **U** know: father, relative, teacher,
Neighbor, doctor, boss, professor, date, fiance, husband,
Compatriot (**75%**); or pervert hiding in bushes (**25%**).

**RAPE: NO CONSENT** (its that simple)
It's no use crying over spilled milk or **SEMEN**...

*Every Woman Has a Story! Find Your Voice! Every Story Counts!*

*2015 ITS ON US.ORG*
*2013 VAWA: Violence Against Women Reauthorization Act*
*MISOGYNY: HATRED OF WOMEN (its that simple)*

Colleges file **FALSE** reports: No campus **R**APES and **MURDER**!
**STIGMATA:** It hurts their reputation and bottom line: **$$$$$**

**SACRIFICIAL LAMB:** R.I.P. Laura Dickinson (EMU 2006)
Settlement: 2.5 Million (Violations: Title IX and Clery Act)

Colleges host fraternity parties who **DRINK, DRUG** & **GANG R**APE
Frat alumni donate millions: **$$$$$** (University **A**PE**S R**APE boys too!)

Yale University Zeta Psi & Delta Kappa Epsilon fraternity chants:
"We Love Yale **SLUTS**" and "No Means Yes! Yes Means Anal!" (YouTube video)

**SACRIFICIAL LAMB** Phi Kappa Psi: Valedictorian Liz Seccuro (UVA 1984)
**GANG R**APE **SURVIVOR**: 22 years later, **R**apist Beebe confesses: "Crash Into Me" (book)

**THE HUNTING GROUND R**ape victims become activists: "**No Jane Doe!**"
129 colleges across nation under investigation: "**RAPE CULTURE**"

**Victim:** Nude, bruised and bloodied; Erica Kinsman stands up and speaks out!
**Victorious:** Florida State University pays Erica Kinsman **$950,000.00**

St. Paul's Preparatory School: One **STUD** muffin is arrested, **BOO HOO**!
Owen Labrie's **SACRIFICIAL LAMB** Chessy Prout is under age, but stood up (5 %)

The "**Senior Salute**" is a high school tradition. Labrie explains,
"Welcome to an eight week exercise in debauchery, a probing
Exploration of the innermost meanings of the word sleazebag."

Under oath, Owen Labrie feigns, "**Divine Inspiration**" BUT two roommates
Out him, "**Divine Intervention**." **SAINTS**: H. Kremer & A. Thomson

Masquerade: Labrie crosses himself before Judge Smukler reads ruling
**STIGMATA: ETERNAL DAMNATION** as sex offender. The **STUD** cries.

Ironically, Labrie lost his 4-year full scholarship to **Harvard Divinity School**
All is not lost: Preach the word of **CHRIST** to fellow convicts- 5 **STIGMATAS**

(C.P) SHE SAID: "No one believes me. I was **R**aped. I'm **SUICIDAL**."
(O.L) HE SAID: "No one believes me. I'm going to jail. I'm **SUICIDAL**."

Labrie's 119 vulgar Facebook messages are noxious fumes that teach
St. Paul's **STUD** muffins (14-17) how to pork, bone, and slay women

**THE HOLY TRINITY: LABRIE** plans, **GOD** laughs, and **DEVIL** takes revenge;
When Labrie is porked, boned, and slayed in jail: **Karmic Justice**

**ICON** Bill Cosby: "**MONSTER**: 50 Allegations Drugged Sexual Assault"
The **LEGEND**: Cancelled, Revoked, Terminated, Arrested: **Poetic Justice**

**RICH WHITE TRASH:** President Donald Trump: "When you're a star, they let
you do it! **Grab Them By The PUSSY**" 12 Accusors✚: **Gloria Allred Justice**

**Children Are Taught:** "Don't Take Candy from Strangers"
**WAKE UP WOMEN:** "Don't Take Alcohol from Anyone"

©All Rights Reserved. Sharon Esther Lampert.

# FAN MAIL

## FANS@SharonEstherLampert.com

### A Letter from Anne Peyton Bryant
### She was One of the Women Attacked in Central Park

Dearest Sharon,

Your words so richly express the disenchantment that this horrifying experience has left upon me. The "concentric circles" you speak of nearly squeazed the life out of me, though I was unaware that these circles even existed until I was violently thrust into the center.

    I recall the first time I read your poem. Frayed at the edges and ready to give in, your perspective on this tragedy served as a vital source of empowerment when I truly needed it the most. Thank you.

    I hope that it continues to serve as a reminder to women who read it that fighting back is the only course of action that will effect a change in our culture --the participants in each circle must take responsibility for their contribution to this tragedy, which is now a wound on my soul that I fear I will never be able to completely heal.

Thank you so much!
Anne Peyton Bryant
**AWARD FOR STANDING UP & STANDING TALL**
**NOW** selected Anne Peyton Bryant as a receipient of the Susan B. Anthony Award to be presented on Feb 20, 2001.

Anne Peyton Bryant

# #1 Poetry Website for Student Projects

## THE GREATEST POEM EVER WRITTEN ON
### Central Park, N.Y.C., Sunday, June 11th, 2000, 11:30 a.m.–6:30 p.m.

# Water Fight, Flight, and Tears

(1) From the five boroughs of N.Y.C., sixty soulless monsters came, not knowing each other, they all found each other in agreement: water all the women with **ICE** and bring them to tears.

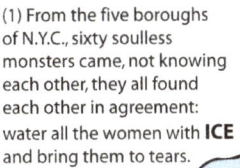

(2) Disarmed, each woman, -fifty and counting, and countless others - is disrobed, robbed, sexually pawed, and clawed. Concentric circles form around a sole woman; a first circle of raging participants; a second circle of cheering and jeering spectators; and a third circle of indifferent police; 4500 police on duty; 900 in the park; eight calls to 911.

(3) Videotapes abound: Sexual Abuse and Violence Against Women. Madams, did it or did it not happen in our park; in the heart of the Big Apple? Men are everywhere but no real men are anywhere to be found: Too afraid: **IMPOTENT** are our men of the possible knife wielding soulless monsters attacking. There are no **HEROES** marching in this Puerto Rican Day Parade on **WOMEN: NADA**

(4) In childhood my father gave me an emergency whistle. Senselessly murdered, crossing Central Park, with the sun at her side, the tragedy of Joan, the beloved daughter of our distinguished Cantor, Jacob Singer, of my synagogue, sent chills down the spines and tears down the cheeks of the choking congregants, whose heart-felt ears heard the horrific news that severed their throats. On that Sabbath prayers went unheard and unanswered. An **ICEBERG**: compassion, mercy, and justice did not exist in that space in that place in the park. A sign must be posted. Where does the **EVIL** come from? Why does cold-blooded, soulless Cain have the wrong right of way to destroy the body and soul of Abel? And why is Abel unable to protect himself from his own demise?

(5) As a young adult, a canister of mace hung from the belt loop of a pant pocket or from my keychain; who knows who lurks behind unopened doors, and the upper east side rapist is still at large and nightly, he is on the prowl. Flyers of his mug hang in every doorway. At 6 a.m., I jog around the placid Central Park Reservoir, not knowing whether I am getting more fit and healthy or am I going to have myself killed.

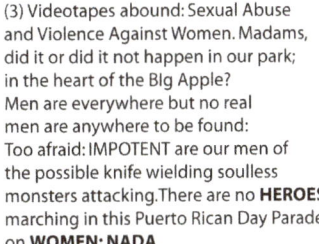

(6) As an adult, in full bloom, it is time, says this breast bearing woman, to bear arms. Nothing less than a gun will protect my sacred soul from the soulless monsters who have no fear of daylight or police and no shame of ganging up on women, children, or the elderly. This remedy places the victimhood on the victimizers, as they are now the victims of their victimization. **JUSTICE WILL BE SERVED COLD.**

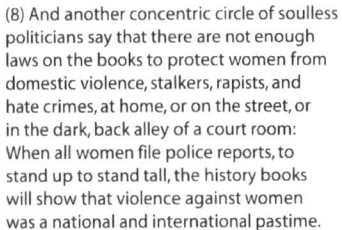

(7) Provoked, even a dog would bite off the hand or chew up the leg of one of these soulless monsters and remain on the right side of the law. Quick on a trigger, a cat would extend its sharpened claws, engraving blood lit scars into each and every face. Defenseless, women do not strike back, unable to poke out the eyes or kick in the groins of any of these soulless monsters.

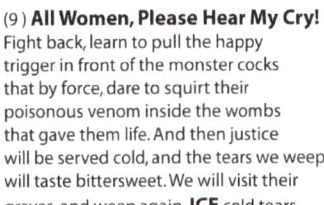

(8) And another concentric circle of soulless politicians say that there are not enough laws on the books to protect women from domestic violence, stalkers, rapists, and hate crimes, at home, or on the street, or in the dark, back alley of a court room: When all women file police reports, to stand up to stand tall, the history books will show that violence against women was a national and international pastime.

(9) **All Women, Please Hear My Cry!**
Fight back, learn to pull the happy trigger in front of the monster cocks that by force, dare to squirt their poisonous venom inside the wombs that gave them life. And then justice will be served cold, and the tears we weep will taste bittersweet. We will visit their graves, and weep again, **ICE** cold tears.

**"The Sole Intention of My Poetry is to Add LIGHT to Your Soul"**
Having handed out this poem to park police and running mates who jog around Central Park, this poem has already inspired women to open up their hearts to me and share with me horrific assaults that they have survived at the hand of violent men who prey on women; and has empowered these same women to find the courage to file their belated police reports. I want this poem to plant a seed in the hearts of all women to fight for their civil right to be protected in their homes and in the streets.

## Sharon Esther Lampert
**Sexiest Creative Genius in Human History**
8th Prophetess of Israel: 22 Commandments
© All Rights Reserved.

### www.PoetryJewels.com
Diamonds, Emeralds, Sapphires, Rubies, and Pearls

# FAN MAIL

## FANS@SharonEstherLampert.com

Date: Thursday, November 19, 2009, 3:11 PM

Dear Ms. Lampert,
Hi
I am doing a poetry project for my English Honors 10th grade class and found your poem, "Simon Wiesenthal: Survivors Burden" and need the date of publication to include it in my project. I am also going to share it with my temple's confirmation class.

Thank you for getting back to me as soon as possible so I can finish my project.

Sincerely,
Josh


## So Special! A Letter from the Simon Wiesenthal Family

From: Joeri Kreisberg
Wednesday, March 29, 2006, 7:43 AM
Poem about Simon Wiesenthal

Dear Ms. Lampert,

I am in receipt of your letter to me with the poem written on my grandfather, Simon Wiesenthal.

First of all, apologies for my belated reply, which so late for various reasons, it has been quite a hectic time.

**We were all very moved to receive the poem, and I made sure to distribute all copies thereof to my sister, Rachel and her husband Yossi and their three girls, Elah, Maya and Tali, to my brother Danny and his wife Orlee and their two children Liron and Shani, and of course to my wife Tamar, and our two boys David and Michael.**

We very much appreciated your kind gesture, and I would like to thank you on behalf of all of us, including my parents, Paullina and Gerard Kreisberg.

All the best,
Joeri Kreisberg
Ramat Gan 52521, Israel

#1 Poetry Website for Student Projects

# WORLD FAMOUS POEMS GREATEST NAZI HUNTER

### THE SOLE INTENTION OF MY POETRY IS TO ADD LIGHT TO YOUR SOUL
## THE GREATEST POEM EVER WRITTEN ON SIMON WIESENTHAL

**Simon Wiesenthal (1908-2005)**

On September 20th, 2005, Simon Wiesenthal died at the age of 96. He was born in the Ukraine. He was trained as an Architect. At age 36, he was liberated from the Mauthausen Concentration Camp. He had been imprisoned in a total of 12 concentration camps (five of which were death camps). He lost 88 relatives in the Holocaust. He married Cyla Muller, a survivor and had a daughter, Dr. Paulina Kreisberg. He has three grandchildren and seven greatgrandchildren. **He dedicated his life to tracking down, hunting, and gathering information on fugitive Nazis to bring them to justice for war crimes and crimes against humanity.**

He received many distinguished awards:
U.S. Congressional Gold Medal (1980)
French Legion of Honor (1986)
Presidential Medal of Freedom (2000)
Honorary British Knighthood (2004)
Austrian Golden Decoration of Merit (2005)

His memoirs and movies are entitled:
"I Hunted Eichmann" (1961)
"The Murderers Among Us" (1967)
"Justice, Not Vengeance: Recollections" (1989)
Academy Award-winning documentary, "Genocide"

**Sharon Esther Lampert**
Sexiest Creative Genius in Human History
8th Prophetess of Israel: 22 Commandments
**www.PoetryJewels.com**
Diamonds, Emeralds, Sapphires, Rubies, and Pearls

Todah Rabah to Karl, My Darling Muse
Written on October 6th, 2005
© All Rights Reserved

A Memorial Tribute in Poetry to Simon Wiesenthal
## A Survivor's Burden

**After six million Jews were silenced:**
Simon speaks above a hush.
Simon speaks above a whisper.
Simon speaks above an earshot.
Simon speaks out loud above the deafening scream of EVIL.

**After six million Jews were silenced:**
Simon's voice shatters the ghetto walls of anti-Semitism.
Simon's voice bellows in the streets of Argentina.
Simon's voice hallows in the halls of JUSTICE.
Simon's voice harkens in the International Arena of INJUSTICE.

**After six million Jews were silenced:**
Simon Wiesenthal WALKS his TALK and JUSTICE is done:
Adolf Eichman is brought to JUSTICE.
Franz Stangl is brought to JUSTICE.
Franz Murer is brought to JUSTICE.
Erich Rajakowitsch is brought to JUSTICE.
Hermine Braunsteiner is brought to JUSTICE.
Karl Silberbauer is brought to JUSTICE.
Josef Schwammberger is brought to JUSTICE.
1,100 Nazi War Criminals are brought to JUSTICE.

**After six million Jews were silenced:**
Simon Says:
"This man is on my list as a suspected war criminal."
Simon Says:
"When history looks back I want people to know the Nazis weren't able to kill millions of people and get away with it."
Simon Says:
"If we don't do anything about evil, that will encourage future perpetrators."
Simon Says:
"My work is a warning for the murderers of tomorrow."
Simon Says:
"Survival is a privilege which entails obligations. I am forever asking myself what I can do for those who have not survived."
Simon Says:
"I have received many honors in my lifetime; when I die, these honors will die with me, but the Simon Wiesenthal Center will live on as my legacy."
Simon Says:
"My epitaph should read simply **"SURVIVOR."**
Simon Says (in the afterlife... to the six million Jews murdered in the Holocaust):
**"I didn't forget you."**

---

**CHILD OF HOLOCAUST SURVIVOR'S BURDEN**
I am a child of a Holocaust survivor...
The "Child of Holocaust Survivor's Burden" is to preserve the memories of the Holocaust survivor.
In this poem, I BEAR WITNESS to keep Simon Wiesenthal's message ALIVE for future generations.
I hope Simon Wiesenthal, the quintessential researcher, is proud of my ability to ferret out the facts of his life.

**NOTES ON THE NAZIS:**
Adolf Eichmann was a planner of Jewish extermination. Fritz Stangl was a commandant of two death camps. Franz Murer was "The Butcher of Wilno." Erich Rajakowitsch was in charge of the "death transports" in Holland. Gestapo officer Karl Silberbauer arrested Anne Frank in her Amsterdam hideout. Hermine Braunsteiner Ryan, helped process the murder of women and children at a camp in Poland and later was found living as a housewife in Queens, N.Y. SS Officer Josef Schwammberger used his German shepherd dog, Prince, to sadistically prey on Jewish inmates.

# LOVE POEMS

For My Love, A.K.

## Rabbi Ari Intimate Blessings

Descending from a long line of orthodox rabbis—the orthodox rabbi appeared
I was an afternoon-conservative Hebrew-school teacher, popular and dear.

We were both children of a Holocaust survivor, unconscious common ground
He was also a therapist, and poking around in my mind, he found
in my philosophical attitude and approach to life, a familiar-haunting sound.

Models date rock stars; actresses date producers; athletes date cheerleaders;

Bosses date secretaries; chefs date waitresses; writers date editors;

Doctors date nurses; dentists date hygienists; therapists date patients;

Pilots date flight attendants; professors date students; sculptors date their nudes;

Nuns don't date their priests; rabbis do date their Hebrew-school teachers.

A boyfriend, I don't remember, a lover he became,
I wasn't emotionally able to play the marriage game.

Only one memory lingers of the covert love affair:
Making love and being wrapped tightly in his arms, is all I can recall—
And where he put his key, he didn't carry on Shabbat, a crevice is in the wall.

I feel infinitely blessed by the long lineage of rabbis in this very intimate setting
Blessings were given, all night long, even if there wasn't going to be a wedding.

I can't recall how the love affair ended, a season at most, it is a mystery, oh dear...
Passions were set aflame and passions were requited in love.

He then set me free, and let me be me...
Ethereal: a celestial being, an angel, from way up above.

—Sharon Esther Lampert
March 3rd, 2004
Special Note of Gratitude to Rabbi Ari, My Muse

For My Love, Dr. K.C.

# FIRST LOVE
**SEE THE WORLD THROUGH THE EYES OF A CREATIVE GENIUS**

As a college freshman, I was relentlessly pursued by an Italian-Catholic boy.

He asked me out to a movie:
I told him I couldn't go because "I AM JEWISH!"
He asked me where I was from: I said, "I AM JEWISH!"
He asked me what my major was: I said, "I AM JEWISH!"
He asked me what I wanted to be when I grow up – I mean graduated!
I said, "I AM JEWISH!"

For three months, he placed love notes into my dorm-room mailbox.
I still have them.

"With love's light wings did I o'er-perch these walls, for stony limits cannot hold love out," said Romeo.

He was brilliant, a Presidential scholar.
He was gorgeous, a member of the basketball team
He came from an all-boys Catholic high school;
I came from a Solomon Schecter Day School.
He said he wanted to convert.

What did he see in me? I had a mouth full of metal braces.
He gave me a button that said, "Tin-Grin." I have that too!

Love notes and all, he became irresistible:
The last image I remember before I got very lost in the throes of ecstasy
was of a wooden statue of JESUS hanging over his bed.
We were all naked.
Two of us were Jews.
Him, Me, JESUS: a Holy Trinity.
He had made me a woman.

Later, I was very miserable over the fact that I was so happy.

"I AM JEWISH…WOMAN!" Mazel Tov!

The nouveau Romeo & Juliet had met each other's parents too!

3 out of 4 parents wished them well—the 4th parent was a Jewish-Holocaust survivor.

"O happy dagger! This is thy sheath; there rust, and let me die," said Juliet.

When he grew up – I mean graduated! – he became, "A Nice-Catholic Doctor"… a Psychiatrist.

I was his first patient! — Parting is Such Sweet Sorrow, said Juliet.

"For never was a story of more woe than this of Juliet and her Romeo," said, William Shakespeare.

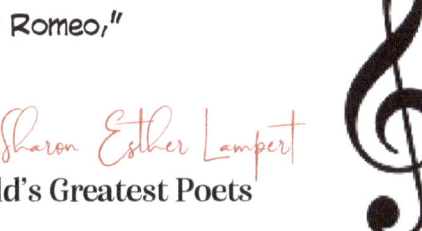

"Tin Grin" *Sharon Esther Lampert*
One of the World's Greatest Poets

For My Love, Y.J. Jacks, United Kingdom, Israeli-Englishman

# THAT KISS

Fortune teller that I AM,
My crystal ball sees ALL.
Clairvoyant, the man's libido is flam**BOY**ant.
I SEE: **ANIMAL MAGNETISM.**
Inside of **THAT KISS** will be BLISS.

Taking chances with amorous glances,
He advances... Lips pouting-tongue tied:
**THAT KISS: SmOOch; smOOch.**
When he romances: his gait prances,
His penis lances, his generosity enhances.
**VOODOO, or DOO-YOU** want dinner, dear?"
His heart dances....

Magician that **HE IS**,
He has a loaded deck of cards,
And wants to be my bodyguard.
Enchantment: a bag of mesmerizing tricks,
An **ACE** up his sleeve, a **KING** or a **JACK**
Are inside of his top hat of black.
Sleight of hand, **THAT KISS** is grand.

**WIZARDRY:** Pressed into his bosom,
I am caught in his embraces, arms
Flailing, like a net above my head,
His pounding heart is beating red.
**THAT KISS** tells **ALL** or just enough
To keep me Interested in **ALL** of his stuff.

Lips full of feelings, **THAT KISS**,
Soft as rose petals, free of prickly thorns.
In the the dark recesses of his mouth,
I find my way by the light in his eyes,
His smile is real, there is no disguise.

Even though we just met,
I am caught in the tangled web of
A hot-blooded, Israeli-Englishman:
"A Jack of All of Love's Trades."
A rare mixed-breed, a British accent,
Concealing a *Sabra, wherever he went.
Tricks of my own trade, I roll up my sleeve,
And I become a woman-in-need(?)
**THAT KISS** I can't forget, and with no regret:
It is almost 4 a.m., and inside of my gypsy's tent:
Sm(**OO**)ch, sm(**OO**)ch,
We are still one silhouette.

**ANIMAL MAGNETISM:**
Sm(**OO**)ch, sm(**OO**)ch,
Some call it v(**OO**)d(**OO**),
Most think it witchcraft,
Experts refer to it as "osculation."
Others call **THAT KISS** Kabbalah;
A kind of Jewish mysticism:
Many are in need of exorcism.

Translation: "Sabra" is a Jew born in Israel.

**Sharon Esther Lampert**
**Sexiest Creative Genius in Human History**
8th Prophetess of Israel: 22 Commandments
Todah Rabah to My Darling Muse Y.J. Jacks
© January 2003, All Rights Reserved.
**www.PoetryJewels.com**
Diamonds, Emeralds, Sapphires, Rubies, and Pearls

For My Love, Dr. J.P.M., Harvard M.D., Half Jewish-Half Arab

# My Man

Making Love All Through the—Night—
and Making Love All Through the—Day

**My Man**
is passionate and strong, all through
the night—I know his emotional,
spiritual, and physical being; I feel
the breadth and depth of his masculinity

All through the night, **My Man** holds
me tightly in his arms: warm, tender,
and cuddly—childlike—always knowing
where I am, secure forevermore

**My Man's** touch lingers—
I am sleeping soundly all
through the night, still making
love with him, in my dreams

I awaken to **My Man's** soft kisses at
dawn, my spirit floating in the morning
mist—the promise of love is fulfilled—
my heart is murmuring a melody, a
sweet new song, all through the day

By Sharon Esther Lampert

@All Rights Reserved. Sharon Esther Lampert.

# NYU Honored Sharon Esther Lampert with an Award for "Multi-Interdisciplinary Studies" (YOUTUBE video)

- Poet
- Prophet
- Philosopher Queen
- Peacemaker
- Princess & Pea
- PINUP
- Performer
- Player: Jock
- Paladin of Education
- PHOTON SUPERHERO
- Princess Kadimah
  8TH Prophetess of Israel
- President
  Smartgrades Brain Power Revolution
- Physicist
- Publisher
- Producer
- Psychobiologist: Rockefeller U.
- Piano-Playing Cat
- Phoenix
- Prodigy

## My Websites:
SharonEstherLampert.com
PhilosopherQueen.com
WorldFamousPoems.com
PoetryJewels.com
GodIsGoDo.com
Schmaltzy.com
TrueLoveBurnsEternal.com
SillyLittleBoys.com
WritersRunTheWorld.com
PalmBeachBookPublisher.com
HappyGrandparenting.com
BooksArePowerful.com

## EDUCATION
Smartgrades.com
EverydayanEasyA.com
PhotonSuperHero.com
BooksNotBombs.com

# SEE THE WORLD THROUGH THE EYES OF A CREATIVE GENIUS

About the Prodigy

## SHARON ESTHER LAMPERT

V.E.S.S.E.L. **V**ery. **E**xtra. **S**pecial. **S**haron. **E**sther. **L**ampert.

**POET** — One of the World's Greatest Poets "A LIST"
**World Poetry Record: 120 Words of Rhyme from One Family of Rhyme**
Greatest Poems Ever Written on Extraordinary World Events

http://famouspoetsandpoems.com/poets.html

### PRODIGY

- Unleash the Creator, The God Within: 10 Esoteric Laws of Genius and Creativity

### PROPHET — GOD IS GO! DO!

- The 22 Commandments: All You Will Ever Need to Know About God
- God Talks to Me: A Working Definition of God

### PHYSICIST AND BIOLOGIST

- God of What? 11 Esoteric Laws of Inextricability, Q: Is Life a Gift or a Punishment?
- Sperm Manifesto: There Is Only Room for One at The Top, 10 Rules for the Road

### PHILOSOPHER QUEEN

- Temporary Insanity: We Are All Building Our Lives on a Sand Trap — Written in Letter **S**
- WOMEN HAVE ALL THE POWER But Have Never Learned How to Use It!

### PEACEMAKER

World Peace Equation

### PHOTON SUPERHERO OF EDUCATION

### PALADIN OF EDUCATION

**SMARTGRADES BRAIN POWER REVOLUTION**
- "The Silent Crisis Destroying America's Brightest Minds"

**BOOK OF THE MONTH, Alma Public Library, Wisconsin**
- EVERYDAY AN EASY A.com
- 40 Universal Gold Standards of Education
- Intra-personal Integration Therapy
- 15 Stepping Stones of Academic Successs
- 15 Stumbling Blocks of Academic Failure

### Pioneer

- SILLY LITTLE BOYS: 40 Rules of Manhood
- LYMTY: Love You More Than Yesterday
  14 Relationship Strategies for Happily Ever After
- In One Hour, Read Hebrew
- CUPID: The Language of Love — Written in Letter **C**
- The Secret Sauce of Book Sales — Written in Letter **P**
- Win at Thin: Fat Me, Skinny Me — Written in Letter **A**

### PIN-UP
SEXIEST CREATIVE GENIUS IN HUMAN HISTORY

# Artists March to the Beat of a Different Drummer
## Sharon Esther Lampert Marches to the Beat of an Entire Orchestra

Poet, Philosopher, Prophet
Paladin of Education, Peacemaker
Princess & Pea, Phoenix, PHOTON, PINUP, Prodigy

Big-Blue-Eyes. Brilliant Books. Beautiful & Buxom. Blessed.

Sharon Esther Lampert was born an **OLD SOUL** — She was never young! Sharon is a lefty.
At age nine, her mother declared: **"My daughter is a poet, philosopher, and teacher!"**
At age nine, Sharon was writing books on memo pads, and binding them together with a stapler.
When Sharon walked into a room, her mother would proclaim, **"THE QUEEN HAS ARRIVED!"**

Her mother nicknamed her daughter, **"The Princess and the Pea!"** Sharon's greatest literary works woke her up in the middle of the night — and made her get up out of bed — and write them down. Sharon writes an entire book in one night! e.g., GOD TALKS TO ME: A WORKING DEFINITION OF GOD

**Sharon's literary genius is to amalgamate poetry, philosophy, and comedy into one sentence.**
Sharon's **BIG BRAIN** conceptualizes **BIG IDEAS** using one letter of the alphabet: **C, S, D** and **P**.
Sharon's mother was the sole person in Sharon's life who knew who Sharon was from the **INSIDE OUT!**

Her beloved mother also knew to her very last breath... the exact day and to-the minute when she would die! (Eve Paikoff Lampert: June 3, 1925 — May 5, 1985).

**Sharon Esther's Gifts Are Metaphysical** — Beyond the Scope of Scientific Inquiry

**There Are No Rough Drafts!** — My Books Write Themselves!
(There Are 4 Books with **God** in the Title)

**"A LIST" Sharon Esther Lampert is One of the World's Greatest Poets**
http://famouspoetsandpoems.com/poets.html

## #1 Poetry Website for Student Projects

On a global scale, Sharon's poetry is used by teachers for their poetry lesson plans, and by students for their poetry projects.

**New York University Awards (YOUTUBE Videos) B.A. M.A. M.A.**

Sharon Esther earned three degrees from NYU — and she was honored with two NYU awards.

Sharon represented her class at her M.A. graduation — and was honored with an award for **"Multi-Interdisciplinary Studies."**

She also played on the NYU Women's Varsity Basketball Team as a Center in the $16-million Coles Sports Center.

Sharon won an "NYU Weightlifting Contest" — Sharon was the sole contestant — so she won! (NYU Washington Square News article).

"When I'm not writing, I'm reading. When I'm not writing or reading, I'm singing." (YOUTUBE videos).
—**Sharon Esther Lampert**

# One of the World's Greatest Poets

http://famouspoetsandpoems.com/poets.html

List of Poets - Famous Poets and Poems            http://famouspoetsandpoems.com/poets.html

 Larry Levis (3) (1946 - 1996)
 Amy Levy (69) (1861 - 1889)
 Louise Labe (1) (1524 - 1566)
 David Lehman (58) (1948 - present)
 Jiri Mordecai Langer (1) (1894 - 1943)
 John Lindley (4) (1952 - present)
 Dimitris Lyacos (3) (1966 - present)
 Yahia Lababidi (10) (1973 - present)

 Laurie Lee (6) (1914 - 1997)
 Walter Savage Landor (52) (1775 - 1864)
 Michael Lally (1) (1942 - present)
 Major Henry Livingston, Jr. (23) (1748 - 1828)
 Roddy Lumsden (2) (1966 - present)
 Sharmagne Leland-St. John (5) (1953 - present)
 **Sharon Esther Lampert (19) (0 - present)**

 M

 Claude McKay (76) (1889 - 1948)
 Spike Milligan (35) (1918 - 2002)
 Marianne Moore (18) (1887 - 1972)
 John Milton (102) (1608 - 1674)
 A. A. Milne (22) (1882 - 1956)
 Czeslaw Milosz (33) (1911 - 2004)
 Edgar Lee Masters (251) (1868 - 1950)
 William Matthews (10) (1942 - 1997)
 Edwin Muir (14) (1887 - 1959)

 Roger McGough (14) (1937 - present)
 Walter de la Mare (44) (1873 - 1956)
 Antonio Machado (8) (1875 - 1939)
 Edna St. Vincent Millay (165) (1892 - 1950)
 W. S. Merwin (23) (1927 - present)
 John Masefield (25) (1878 - 1967)
 Louis MacNeice (3) (1907 - 1963)
 Thomas Moore (144) (1779 - 1852)
 Christopher Marlowe (6) (1564 - 1593)

## What Happens When You Dress Up Albert Einstein As Marilyn Monroe?
### SHARON ESTHER LAMPERT

### SEE THE WORLD THROUGH THE EYES OF A CREATIVE GENIUS

# FAN MAIL
## FANS@SharonEstherLampert.com

# FAN MAIL
FANS@SharonEstherLampert.com

Dear Sharon,

You are not only an exquisite poet, you're beautiful! Am smitten by your luminous beingness. Are you an angel in disguise--a so-called malachim in Hebrew if I am not mistaken.

Thank you for your wondeful open-hearted response.

**Your photo will sit next to those of Gautama Buddha and the Blessed Virgin Mary.**

I will follow your sound esoteric advise regarding the positioning of your photo and the two other icons.

I am deeply impressed that you are very conscious about the concept of sacred space and the flow of spiritual energy.

So please send me your precious photo as soon as possible.

P.S. Will you be generous enough to send me your signed photo which I will place on the secret altar of my heart, lit by the menorah, the seven-stemmed candelabra of your inspiration, O mystical muse, O Rose of Sharon...

Your ardent fan and admirer,

—Felix Fojas, the cybercat with a mystical meow
Chico, CA, 95926

# FAN MAIL

## FANS@SharonEstherLampert.com

*Congregation Emanu-El*
*of the City of New York*
*Fifth Avenue at Sixty-fifth Street*
*New York, N.Y. 10021-6596*

*Study of*
**DAVID M. POSNER**

September 22, 1999

The New York Public Library
Humanities and Social Sciences Library
Fifth Avenue and 42nd Street
New York, NY 10018-2788

Dear Friends:

Sharon Esther Lampert has made application for a fellowship from the Center for Scholars and Writers. It is with greatest pleasure that I write to you in support of her application.

I can best describe this remarkable woman by citing the analysis of Moses Maimonides, in his "Guide for the Perplexed," concerning psychological endowments. He noted the class of people who are intellectually superior, but whose imaginative faculties are deficient. These, he said, were philosophers. Then there are those whose imaginative faculties are highly developed, but who are deficient intellectually. He said these are dreamers and politicians. But then he observed the rare people who have both highly developed intellects and imaginations. These, he said, are prophets.

Sharon Esther Lampert falls into the last category. She has one of the most gifted intellects I have ever encountered, and her imaginative capacity is absolutely awesome.

I have known many people throughout my long career at Temple Emanu-El. I have never met anyone like this extraordinary human being.

Again, awesome is the most appropriate word.

Yours truly,

FORMED BY THE CONSOLIDATION OF EMANU-EL CONGREGATION AND TEMPLE BETH-EL

# #1 Poetry Website
## for Student Projects

# FAN MAIL
## FANS@SharonEstherLampert.com

Windsor High School
6208 Hwy 61-67
Imperial, Mo 63052

SAINT LOUIS MO 631
27 MAY 05 PM

Sharon Esther Lampert
P.O.BOX 103,
New York, New York,10028,US

Cody Howell
1042 Prospect Dr.
Imperial, Mo 63052
May 2, 2005

Sharon Esther Lampert
P.O.BOX 103,
New York, New York,10028,US

    Dear, Sharon E. Lampert

Hello, My name in Cody, I am a Junior at Windsor High School in Missouri. I have had the chance to write to any one person and I picked you. I have always enjoyed quotes and sayings. Theirs just something about it, like I have always known there is a "better way" but never really found anything until I started to pay attention that their was more than just physical happenings. The poet has the ability to drink from streams science has yet to discover. I used to always reads one liners like
" a community begins to grow when old men plant trees they know they will never enjoy the shade of." Things like this really interested me. Something more than what I had known.

    I am very curious by nature, and this kind of wisdom/intellect really hit the spot for me, now I have many poems, sayings, quotes ext. I can't recite them by heart but I thourouly enjoyed the ones I read. I didn't know of you until me and my buddy were talking about how we like psychology and basically more than average and the "better way". After reading some of your quotes I realized you must have seen your share of happenings and become very wise over the years of thought, poetry, and life.

    My first thought was to write to you and try to flatter you because I enjoyed your work. Well I guess you made your poetry your work. Then I started thinking that this well of knowledge , all that stuff you've learned, it would be a long shot but my curiosity wouldn't stop unless if I asked you if you could share some of the knowledge you have gained. Any and all would be appreciated and probably useful later considering I am still just a 17-year-old kid. I can't think of any other word than greedy, but you have already thought so many with your influences, and I ask you to help me out, If your busy you have already done more than enough, thank you, and thanks for your time while reading this. I am sorry but I always find myself looking for more and I'm positive you have gained useful info in your day. I could imagine the child who has heard many stories, lesions, and wisdoms of many. He'd be one of the most diverse ,intelligent humans around, and with something like this in mind how could I not be greedy.

    I have already learned some from Internet, friends like the one who told me about poems, and family. I have tried to learn patience from the impatient, kindness from the angry, and truth from fools, but for some reason I'm not thankful for these teachers. I still feel as if I could have more, and the lessons of an older experienced poet just has something about how it sounds. Greatness is all I've seen come from poets their ability to make one think is amazing , I could just imagine the wisdom of an experienced one.

    Either way I just wanted to say thank you for your time and thank you for doing what you have done. Your shared wisdom and lessons will help many and your work might not be remembered forever but I believe that your positive effect will. Thank you again

    Your student ,
    Cody

Date: Thursday, November 19, 2009, 3:11 PM

Dear Ms. Lampert,
I am working on a poetry project for my senior English class. Instead of a boring research paper we are to analyze a famous poet and make a power point, and a creative presentation over the poets life, work and also criticisms of their work. The last part is the problem, I can't seem to find any scholarly criticisms of your work. Do you know of any, or have on record any criticisms of your work, either oral or written? My project partner and I would love to do our project on you because we find you very interesting and your poems very in tune with the lives of people today and the problems we face as modern people. Any help would be appreciated.
Thank you again.
Sincerely,
—Michael Rockey

Date: April 10, 2009 6:15:32 PM

Hi Sharon!
My name is Alexa & I'm a junior in high school! I love your poems, especially about world affairs. I will be doing a poetry analysis on three of your poems **(I've chosen Sandstorm in Iraq, Tsunami, and There Is No Flower in Darfur)** and also a presentation to inform the class of your works, accomplishments & biography. I have been searching every website and library on some information about you, but can't find any! If you can it would be greatly appreciated if you could tell me a little about your childhood, parents, education, religious beliefs, and maybe some experiences that have shaped your views or positions in regards to your poetry!
Thanks so much!
Have an amazing day!
—Alexa Young

Date: January 20, 2010 9:54:04 PM

Hello Miss Lampert,
My name is Kal Marshall, I am a student at Johnson City High School, Johnson City, New York. I am currently enrolled in AP English and Literature. My teacher realized my classes misunderstanding for poetry and decided to have us write paper on a poem of our choice and about the poet. While searching the web for an interesting poem I came among yours and knew it was the poem I was meant to write a paper on. One part of the paper is to "Interview" someone who has read the poem. While I was on your website I found the little note about E-mailing you. So I was wondering if you would be willing to give me a little more detail on your poem, **"EDUCATE NOT."** From the basis under which it was derived from, to your true feeling and understanding of the poem, to how you feel about it now from when you were writing it. Your Bio is extremely interesting, and I hope to learn more. Thank you very much for creating a poem I could actually enjoy to spend a month working on. and hopefully I hear back from you in a reasonable time.
Thanks Again,
—Kal Marshall

# Gazillions...
## National & International Poetry Publications

### Afghanistan: RAHA
2003:
Princess Kadimah is Published in Afghanistan: RAHA
Dear Sharon
I added you to my list and also your work is published on the net:
http://rahapen.org/options_poetry_Sharon.htm
Regards
—Kamran Mirhazar
Raha PEN Club
Email: rahapen@kabulpress.org
0093-799390025
Kabul, Afghanistan:  Post Box number: 3219

Dear Sharon Esther Lampert,
Your artistic poem CENTRAL PARK: Water Fight, Flight and Tears
marked by true creative genius,
has been published in the June of Taj Mahal Review an International
Literary Journal ISSN  0972-6004.
This Journal contains 300 pages of short stories, literary articles and
poems by authors from all over the world.
The Journal is an attempt to select the best of world poetry.
Best Wishes
—RADHA AGRAWAL
www.cyberwit.net
4/2 B, L.I.G.
Govindpur Colony Allahabad - 211004 (U.P.)
INDIA

Dear Sharon,
When we made our recent call for submissions, in which we asked for writings pertaining to the terrorist attacks of September 11, 2001, we were unsure what kind of response we would get.  As it turns out, we have received poetry, fiction, and essays from writers all over the world.  Our "feature writer section" for October will include the work of over 100 writers.  We are very happy to include your work in this section. Your contribution to this project is an integral part of the overall tone and spirit of the October issue.  We want to thank you for helping us in this project and, more importantly, expressing yourself at a time when to do so is both difficult and essential. Thank you again for sending us your work.
The October issue will come out on October 21, 2001.
 Sincerely,
 The Pedestal Magazine
  www.thepedestalmagazine.com

Sharon, Thanks for the note.  I really appreciate it.  A gift, huh?  Wow, I am intigued and flattered. By the way, several people really liked your writing in the current Pedestal.
Best,
—John Amen

# Gazillions...
**National & International Poetry Publications**

**Dear Sharon,**
Thank you so much for the kind comments.
I am pleased to have your poems Timeless Sandcastles and Sacred Feathers Of Divine Freedoms appearing in the first issue of Thought Fragments.
I will send you a reminder email when the first issue goes up.
Once again, thank you.
Best wishes,
—Darlene Zagata

Featured Poem of the Month:
Cool...thanks!
It's a pleasure to feature your work.
I want you to know that i have a lot of respect and admiration for Jewish people.
I look forward to learning more about you and your culture through your work.
—Nate

Dear Sharon,
Several weeks ago we informed you by mail that our editors wish to include your poetry in a new collection of poems written by the Best poets we have encountered. We need to hear back from you immediately if you wish to be included in the special edition . . .
The Best Poems and Poets of 2002
Library of Congress ISBN 0-7951-5175-6

Dear Sharon,
My name is August Highland - i am a writer and editor - i read your work
i dream forge - i like your work - a lot - i want to include your work in the next issue of the little literary -journal of which i am the editor - you can see the muse apprentice guild at www.muse-apprentice-guild.com - internet explorer 5.5 or higher is required send me as many pieces as you like sharon and they can be of any
length - also include a short bio
Always,
—August

Dear Sharon,
We have discussed this at length and have concluded that your
poems are truly unique and rather exciting.
Fondly,
—Ruby M.
Editor, PrinsessTarta Magazine

Sharon,
How do we get your poem into my site?
—Richard Williams, Editor

# World Famous Quotes

## THERE IS ONE GLOBAL ENEMY: IGNORANCE
—PHOTON SUPERHERO OF EDUCATION

## LONELINESS IS DEATH
## SOLITUDE IS DIVINE

—Philosopher Queen Sharon Esther Lampert

## BE HARD
## ON A WOMAN ONLY WHEN MAKING LOVE TO HER

—Philosopher Queen Sharon Esther Lampert

## FIGHT TO LIVE
## LIVE TO FIGHT
## BORN TO DIE

—Philosopher Queen Sharon Esther Lampert

## THERE IS ONLY ONE TRUTH
## NO ONE HAS THE TRUTH

—Philosopher Queen Sharon Esther Lampert

# World Famous Quotes

## EVERY THOUGHT IN YOUR HEAD WAS PUT THERE BY A WRITER

— Prodigy Sharon Esther Lampert

## THE 11 COMMANDMENT
## KEEP THEM LAUGHING
## KEEP THEM SANE

### There Are 5 Books of Moses and 5000 Books of Jewish Comedy

—Princess Kadimah, 8TH Prophetess of Israel

## GOD IS GO! DO!
### God Can Only Do for You What God Can Do Through You

God Is Not Physics — The Laws of the Universe
God is Metaphysics — Beyond the Scope of Scientific Inquiry
An Invisible and Intangible Entity Like Your Mind, Thoughts, and Ideas

### Less Than 1% Population and 22% Nobel Prizes
## Wherever Jews Go, Grass Grows
## Wherever Israelis Go, Gardens Grow

—Princess Kadimah, 8TH Prophetess of Israel

# KADIMAH PRESS: Gifts of Genius
## Revelations! My Books Write Themselves!

**18 BOOKS OF POETRY**
Poet: The Greatest Poems Ever Written on Extraordinary World Events
Title: I Stole All the Words from the Dictionary
#1 Poetry Website for School Projects
A List: One of the World's Greatest Poets
ISBN Hardcover: 978-1-885872-06-7
ISBN Paperback: 978-1-885872-07-4
ISBN E-Book: 978-1-885872-08-1

Prodigy: WORLD PREMIERE!
Title: Unleash the Creator The God Within
10 Esoteric Laws of Genius and Creativity
ISBN Hardcover: 978-1-885872-21-0
ISBN Paperback: 978-1-885872-22-7
ISBN E-Book: 978-1-885872-23-4

Prophet: WORLD PREMIERE! **GOD IS GO! DO!**
Title: GOD TALKS TO ME: A WORKING DEFINITION OF GOD
ISBN Hardcover: 978-1-885872-33-3
ISBN Paperback: 978-1-885872-34-0
ISBN E-Book: 978-1-885872-36-4

Prophet: WORLD PREMIERE!
Title: The 22 Commandments: All You Will Ever Need to Know About God
A Universal Moral Compass For All People, For All Religions, For All Time
ISBN Hardcover: 978-1-885872-03-6
ISBN Paperback: 978-1-885872-04-3
ISBN E-Book: 978-1-885872-05-0

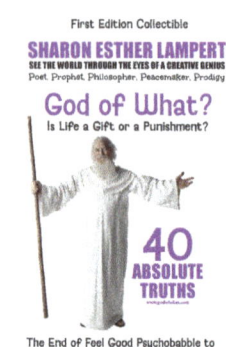

Philosopher Queen: WORLD PREMIERE!
Title: God of What? Is Life a Gift or a Punishment? 10 Absolute Truths
ISBN Hardcover: 978-1-885872-00-5
ISBN Paperback: 978-1-885872-01-2
ISBN E-Book: 978-1-885872-02-9
GodofWhat.com

# KADIMAH PRESS: Gifts of Genius

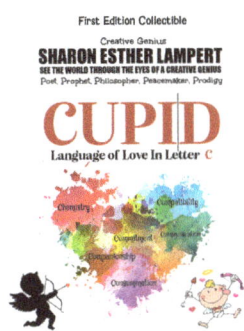

**Prodigy: WORLD PREMIERE!**
Title: CUPID: The Language of Love—Written in Letter C
ISBN Hardcover: 978-1-885872-55-5
ISBN Paperback: 978-1-885872-56-2
ISBN E-Book: 978-1-885872-57-9
SharonEstherLampert.com

**Prodigy: WORLD PREMIERE!**
Title: TEMPORARY INSANITY
We Are All Building Our Lives on a Sand Trap — Written in Letter S
ISBN Hardcover: 978-1-885872-70-8
ISBN E-Book: 978-1-885872-71-5
SharonEstherLampert.com

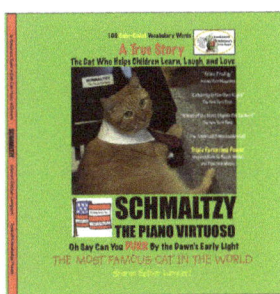

**Popular: Children's Book, Ages 8-12**
Title: SCHMALTZY: IN AMERICA, EVEN A CAT CAN HAVE A DREAM
ISBN Hardcover: 978-1-885872-39-5
ISBN Paperback: 978-1-885872-38-8      **Color-Coded**
ISBN E-Book: 978-1-885872-37-1          Vocabulary Words
Schmaltzy.com
WORLD FAMOUS PIANO PLAYING CAT

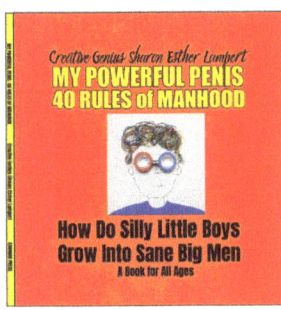

**Popular: WORLD PREMIERE**
Title: 40 RULES OF MANHOOD
HOW DO SILLY LITTLE BOYS GROW INTO SANE BIG MEN
14 Global Catastrophes of Violence Against Women
ISBN Hardcover: 978-1-885872-29-6
ISBN Paperback: 978-1-885872-35-7
ISBN E-Book: 978-1-885872-41-8
SillyLittleBoys.com

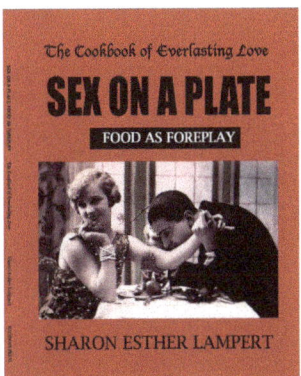

**Popular: Every Relationship Begins with a Great Meal**
Title: SEX ON A PLATE: FOOD AS FOREPLAY
THE COOKBOOK OF EVERLASTING LOVE
ISBN Hardcover: 978-1-885872-46-3
ISBN Paperback: 978-1-885872-48-7
ISBN E-Book: 978-1-885872-47-0
TrueLoveBurnsEternal.com

## Count Your Blessings. Practice Gratitude

### "Never Underestimate the Power of a Girl with a Book"
—ICON Supreme-Court Justice Ruth Bader Ginsburg

### 1. MY GENETIC GIFT OF GENIUS
- Lefty: Born with an Extra Body Part, "**C**reative **A**pparatus"
- Two Sets of Artsy-Fartsy Genes: Maternal Grandfather Benjamin Paikoff and Father Abraham Lampert
- Vocalist: Ashira Orchestra (YOUTUBE videos)
- Athlete: NYU Women's Varsity Basketball Team

### 2. MY LIFE: Dawn of Digital Revolution
- The Golden Age of Personal Computers: APPLE
- The Golden Age of Creativity: ADOBE
- The Golden Age of Email, Internet, and Globalization

NYU President Andrew Hamilton and Me

**NYU Special Mention**
NYU President John Brademas (backed his limosine into my bicycle)
Professor Yael Feldman (the writer's relationship to MOMMY)
Professor Paul Humphreys (class on family therapy)
Professor Ted Coons, (my position at Rockefeller University)
John, The Security Guard at Coles Sports Center (SUPERFAN)
NYU B-Ball Coaches: Evelyn Hannon and Sherri Pickard

### 3. MY LOVED ONES:
- UNCONDITIONAL TRUE LOVE: MOMMY
- MY PURRfect Children: SCHMALTZY & FALAFEL  Schmaltzy.com (YOUTUBE videos)
- My Muse: NYU Professor Karl Bardosh "Friends First and Forever and Family"
- My Metaphysical Sister: Poet Hannah Senesh: "ELI, ELI"

### 4. MY EDUCATION: BA, MA, MA and Awards  (YOUTUBE videos)
- NYU MENTOR: Laurin Raiken: NYU "**Multi-Interdisciplinary Award**" and **MA Class Representative**
- ROCKEFELLER UNIVERSITY, NYC, Publication: "Hyperphagia and Obesity Induced by Neuropeptide Y"
- 100-Year Scholarship Award Winner, Presented by NYC Mayor Edward Koch
- Empire Science Scholarship Award Winner
- Jerusalem Fellowship Award of Aish Hatorah
- Won a Weightlifting Contest, NYU Coles Sports Center (Washington Square News)
- My Egaliterian Childhood: Solomon Schecter Day Schools and Jewish Theological Seminary of America

NYU Professor Karl Bardosh and Me

### 5. MY SPORTS:
- NYC Marathon
- Basketball: NYU Women's Varsity Basketball Team, Center
- Basketball: NYC Urban Professional League
- Skiing: Heavenly, Lake Tahoe, Nevada
- Tennis: Central Park Tennis Courts
- Baseball: Coach Sandy Pyonin
- Hall of Fame Baseball Players: Jean Harding and Wilma Briggs

### 6. MY INSPIRATIONS:
- ISRAEL: "AM YISRAEL CHAI!"  Sheep to Slaughter to Light of the World!
- Rabbi David Posner, Temple Emanu-El NYC, "President of My Fan Club"
- NYC: Personal Freedom & Creative Freedom

NYU Professor Laurin Raiken and Me

# South Florida Sun-Sentinel

DELRAY BEACH NEWS    PALM BEACH COUNTY NEWS

## Spirituality workshop supports A Walk on Water fund

MARCI SHATZMAN MSHATZMAN@TRIBPUB.COM   |   JAN 20, 2016

Sharon Esther Lampert didn't bring her tiara when she moved here from New York, but she found one just in time to be one of the speakers at Barbara M. Wolk's second annual Spirituality Workshop Jan. 24.

"Barbara has this wonderful event in support of autistic children," said Lampert, an author, poet, philosopher and educator who plays a princess for her talks.

She expects to hand out her "30 Commandments: All You Ever Need to Know," at the workshop from 10:30 a.m. to 12:30 p.m. at the Shirley & Barton Weisman Community Center, 7091 W. Atlantic Ave., in Delray Beach.

Admission is a minimum of $10 and the event opens at 10 a.m. A live auction will include a sculpture called "Balance."

# FAN MAIL
## FANS@SharonEstherLampert.com

POEM: "THE PALESTIAN TODDLER TERRORIST"

Wow. So powerful. I so respect your amazing power to express the essence of why the hate exists. You, Sharon, take the reality of hate and express it in literary or poetic format with skill and emotional impact by the juxtaposition of two conflicting ideologies. I met Mosab Hussan Yousef as well. I have deep respect for his courage! Your poem explains why the Hamas war exists!
— Dr. Myles Krieger
2024

Hello, hello, hello Sharon! Florence Spiro calling...
Sharon, I hope that the poem that you sent me about Palestinian children terrorist, oh my God! I hope that millions of people could read that. I wish that all the Palestinians could read that - because it has the potential for opening the eyes and minds of people. Hopefully, potentially, what these Palestinians are doing to the minds - how they corrupting the minds of their children - stealing their children's lives.
**Oh my God brilliant!**
I have been reading the poem to friends and family and sharing the poem and asking people to look it up online.
**Brilliant, brilliant work!**
You have made an important contribution!
So I hope that your poem Is publicized. I will speak to you.
**You are a brilliant woman!**
I'll speak to you my dear Shana Tova , and may there be peace..."
— Florence Spiro
October 2024

# WORLD FAMOUS POEMS
## The Greatest Poems Ever Written on Extraordinary World Events
www.WorldFamousPoems.com

January 15, 2022
## RUN SAID RABBI
Congregation Beth Israel, Colleyville Texas

A cup of tea 🍵
A slice of pizza 🍕
A can of soda
A chair
A British national 🇬🇧
An Islamic meshuganah
A Pakistani anti-Semite ☪️
A lone-wolf 🐺 psychopath

Malik travels 5000 miles ...
Takes four Jewish hostages
In the state of Texas 🤠
At Beth Israel, Colleyville 🕍
FBI negotiations: 11 hours ⏰
Meshuganah said: **"Get on your knees!"**
Rabbi Charlie Cytron-Walker said: **"No!"**

We were not freed or rescued
We escaped inching ... towards ...
the exit door ... 🚪 as meshuganah
put gun down to sip on his soda
Rabbi threw chair
Rabbi Charlie said: **"Run!"** 🏃
L'Chaim! 🍷

FBI fired all bullets 🔫
One less meshuganah in world 🌍
Today feels lighter and brighter! 🌞
LChaim! 🍷

SEE THE WORLD
THROUGH THE EYES OF
A CREATIVE GENIUS

- Prodigy
- Prophet
- Philosopher
- Poet
- Paladin of Education
- Peacemaker
- Princess Kadimah
- PHOTON SUPERHERO
- PINUP
- Princess & Pea
- Phoenix

SHARON ESTHER LAMPERT
PRINCESS KADIMAH
8TH PROPHETESS OF ISRAEL
### GOD IS GO! DO!
THE 22 COMMANDMENTS

The **Sole** Intention of My **Poetry** Is to Add **LIGHT** to Your **Soul**
Sharon Esther Lampert    FANS@SharonEstherLampert.com

# FAN MAIL
## FANS@SharonEstherLampert.com

**Megan Hiles** November 22 at 11:14pm Report
I did a school poetry project on you!!

**Sharon Lampert** November 22 at 11:23pm
Dear Megan Hiles,

Hello.

I am delighted to hear from you.

Thank you so much choosing my poems for your school project. Which poems did you choose?

Enclosed is a gift of poetry: World Peace Equation.

Sharon Esther Lampert
Poet, Philosopher, Peacemaker, Pioneer, Paladin of Education and Prophet

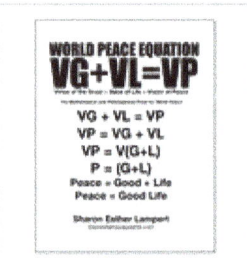

**Megan Hiles** November 22 at 11:32pm Report
I used my fathers garden, impossibe, tsunami, god created abortion and sandstorm in iraq. my teached was impressed that i picked such a up to date poet and philosopher.

Sent via Facebook Mobile

**Sharon Lampert** November 22 at 11:52pm
Dear Megan Hiles,

WOW! What an interesting assortment of poems: family poem, love poem, natural disaster poem, social issue poem, and political poem ... all together in one school project.

Thank you again for choosing my poems for your school project.

Enclosed is another gift of poetry: True Love

Sharon Esther Lampert
Poet, Philosopher, Peacemaker, Pioneer, Paladin of Education and Prophet

**Aviva Lerer** May 18
Is sharon esther lampert jewish? I need to know this for a school project :) Thanks!

#1 Poetry Website for Student Projects
# WORLD FAMOUS POEMS.COM
### The Greatest Poems Ever Written on Extraordinary World Events

## **DEAD**ICATION

**V.E.S.S.E.L.**

Every single second of the day
A suffering is taking place
**Shake-Me. Wake-Me. Save Me.**

Every single second of the day
My belief in a God is shaken
**Shake-Me. Wake-Me. Save Me.**

Death is a greater force than life
Doctors can't heal death
**Shake-Me. Wake-Me. Save Me.**

Evil is a greater force than good
Good cannot vanquish evil — only evil can vanquish evil
You cannot negotiate with evil
Destroy the evil or be destroyed by the evil
**Shake-Me. Wake-Me. Save Me.**

Good deeds are fragile glass
Evil deeds are solid rock
**Shake-Me. Wake-Me. Save Me.**

Good people nothing is a problem
Bad people everything is a problem
**Shake-Me. Wake-Me. Save Me.**

There are no **BELIEVERS**
There are only make-believers and non-believers
Which one are you? A make-believer or a non-believer?
How do you live a moral life in an immoral universe?
**Shake-Me. Wake-Me. Save Me.**

We are born without our consent
We are born ignorant, unconscious, and irrational
We are born this way! We will live this way! We will die this way!
**BLIND LEAD THE BLIND**
**Shake-Me. Wake-Me. Save Me.**

Generations of drama, trauma, and karma
Broken world of broken people
Joy dissipates... Pain endures...
**Shake-Me. Wake-Me. Save Me.**

## GOD IS **DEAD**

## You Cannot Negotiate with Evil
## Destroy the Evil or Be Destroyed by the Evil

### Prophet Sharon Esther Lampert

## Education Cannot Amelioriate Anti-Semitism
## Haters Hate the Facts, the Truth, and the Light

### Prophet Sharon Esther Lampert

## President Biden Wants to Defend Against Terrorism But Does Not Want to Defeat Terrorism
## President Bush Wanted to Defeat Terrorism
## He Wanted to Defeat the Terrorists on Their Turf

### Prophet Sharon Esther Lampert

#1 Poetry Website for Student Projects
# WORLD FAMOUS POEMS.COM
### The Greatest Poems Ever Written on Extraordinary World Events
## Dumb Dee Dee Dumb Dumb

Sitting on Their Ass
On the College Grass

Reciting Toxic Racist Rhymes
Ripping Down Hostage Posters

Don't Know What is Hamas?
Don't Know What River or Sea?

Don't Know Any Terrorist Victims
From 40 Countries of All Faiths!

Hidden Faces in Striped Keffiyahs
Hilarious Queers for Palestine!

Wearing Green HAMAS Headbands
Waving Yellow HEZBOLLAH Flags

**Sharon Esther Lampert**

GENIUS: The Gift of Divine Revelation
Scientist, Artist, Educator, Theologian
FANS@SharonEstherLampert.com

Burning American Flags — Born Before 911, 2001 — Don't Know Osama bin Laden
Don't Know That the Only **FREE ARABS** Live in the Democratic State of **ISRAEL** (Jewish New Year 5785)
1. Freedom of Religion
2. Minority Rights
3. Women's Rights

Don't Know that Entire Middle East Countries are Hijacked by Islamic-Jihad Terrorist Organizations
Iranian Republic Puppets: Gaza, West Bank, Lebanon, Yemen, Iran, Afghanistan, Syria, and Iraq

Don't Know Fact or Fiction, Truth or Lie, or Light Over Darkness (Jedi Over Darth Vader)
Don't Know **TERRORIST CELLS** are Everywhere: "Death to Canada" "Death to UK" "Death to Australia" "Death to USA"

Don't Know that Girls Can't Go to School in Afghanistan — and Can't Remove a Hijab! (UNICEF: 130 Million Girls Worldwide)
Sitting on Their Ass on the College Grass — Don't Know That Every Story Is the Same Story of "Cain and Abel"

Jewish Students are Refused Entry into their Campus Library
Student Protesters "Iranian Useful Idiots" are Arrested and Suspended

Jews: 225+ Nobel Prizes
Jewish Women: 20 Nobel Prizes
Muslims: 15 Nobel Prizes

Vandalized School Property
Disrespected Law Enforcement

Locked Out of College and Dorm
Locked Out of Dining Room

Waste of an Education! Flunked History!
Waste of Parent's Tuition Dollars

Ivy League Presidents Resign
Failed Moral Clarity or Moral Rot Test
Q: Does Calling for the Genocide of Jews Violate
  School Policy?  A: "Its a Matter of Context!"

Don't Know **ZIONISTS** are at the Forefront of
Science, Medicine, Technology, and AI — and
Earned 23% of Nobel Prizes and Every Prize
in Every Field! **ISRAEL Has 13 Nobel Prizes!**

Don't Know Two Billion Muslims Earned
15 Nobel Prizes — **One Was a Terrorist!**

Sitting on Their Ass On the College Grass
**DUMB DEE DEE DUMB DUMB**

## Dumb Dee Dee Dumb Dumb!

# EVERY THOUGHT IN YOUR HEAD WAS PUT THERE BY A WRITER
— Sharon Esther Lampert

I Am **M**ortal.
My Books Are **I**mmortal.
Please Handle My Books Gently.
My Books Are My Remains.

This book was compiled in three parts.
Part 1. Birth of Poet — Age 9-Present
Part 2. Format Book — June 11-12, 2022
Part 3. Publish — August 18, 2022, Update 2024

## Sharon Esther Lampert
**SEE THE WORLD THROUGH THE EYES OF A CREATIVE GENIUS**
**P**oet, **P**rophet, **P**hilosopher, **P**eacemaker, **P**rincess & **P**ea, **P**rodigy

### FAIR USE NOTICE
There are a few copyrighted materials whose use has not been specifically authorized by the copyright owner. We are making this material available in its efforts to advance the understanding of poetry, philosophy, spirituality, and education. We believe this constitutes a 'fair use' of the copyrighted material as provided for in Section 107 of the US Copyright Law.

www.ingramcontent.com/pod-product-compliance
Lightning Source LLC
Chambersburg PA
CBHW051349110526
44591CB00025B/2953